MW00934458

Life in a Rotten Log

Kathie Atkinson

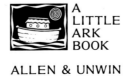

A LITTLE ARK BOOK

ALLEN & UNWIN

The death of a tree

When a tree crashes down in the forest, you might think that's the end of the tree's story. In fact it's not the end, just the start of a new chapter. The tree is dead, but it slowly becomes a rotting log and continues to play an important part in the life of the forest.

Of course things will never be the same as before. Animals living in the tree have their lives turned upside down. Birds lose their nests. Insects and spiders high in the branches suddenly find themselves on the ground. A Feathertail Glider sleeping in its nest-hollow is shaken awake and flees into the forest to find a new home high in another tree.

But these old homes won't be empty for long. Different tenants—animals and plants—will soon move in. Some will make great changes to the log. Others will use it as a hunting ground, or a safe place for themselves and their babies.

Take a close look at life in a rotten log, and see how the story unfolds...

▽ *This tiny Feathertail Glider was asleep in its tree-hollow when the old tree crashed to the ground. Dazed and frightened, it fled into the forest to find a new home.*

New tenants

After dark, the forest comes alive with nocturnal hunters searching for their next meal. As they move about, some of them find the wreckage of the newly fallen tree and quickly make use of it.

A Small-eyed Snake with a full belly finds the glider's old nest-hole. This will be a safe place for the snake to sleep for a few days, while it digests its meal.

Moonlight shines through the gap where the tree used to stand, so the forest floor is brighter than usual. Several small animals nervously explore the churned-up soil beside the broken trunk.

A Dusky Antechinus finds the body of a cricket that was killed in the upheaval, and gobbles it up. This tiny carnivore is only the size of a mouse, but it has a big appetite. It uses its strong claws to forage around the log, pouncing on any spiders and insects it uncovers.

DID YOU KNOW?

Nocturnal animals sleep during the daylight hours and come out at night to feed.

Carnivores are animals that eat the flesh of other animals. (**Herbivores** eat plants.)

Marsupials are mammals that carry their babies in a pouch until they are big enough to look after themselves. Gliders, antechinuses, possums and wombats are marsupials you might see in a forest like this.

A snake curls up in the glider's old home—a safe place to sleep off its last meal. ▽

▷ *A marsupial mouse, called a Dusky Antechinus, hunts for food around the fallen tree trunk.*

4

The under-cover workers

Millipedes and slaters crawling through the leaf litter find the log and wriggle under it. Their new home will give them plenty of rotting vegetation to eat and lots of damp places to hide in. It won't be long before other small creatures join them.

Any insects from the treetop that can't find a place to hide down here on the ground are in real danger. They will soon be eaten by centipedes, beetles and other hunters.

△ Millipedes find food, and damp, dark places to hide under the log.

▽ Pillbugs (slaters) need damp places to live. If you uncover them they roll into little balls to protect themselves.

△ *A ground beetle explores the new log, looking for a meal.*

▷ *This centipede is a fierce hunter. It slips into cracks in the log to find spiders, insects and even other centipedes. The victims can't escape its poisonous fangs.*

8

Some old residents of the tree trunk, like these Huntsman Spiders, don't notice much difference when they squeeze out from under the peeling bark. But they will have to watch out for new predators exploring the fallen log.

When a hungry Johnny Hairylegs Centipede, with long legs and feelers, comes groping about in their space, the spiders escape and scurry off to find somewhere else to live.

By dawn, animals from the night shift have disappeared. Some, like the millipedes and centipedes, hide away safely in the log's dark crevices. Others have returned to their nests in the forest.

◁ *This kind of centipede is called Johnny Hairylegs, because of its extra long, fine legs.*

▽ *Huntsman Spiders have very flat bodies, so they can hide in tight places between the bark and the tree trunk.*

DID YOU KNOW?

Predators hunt other animals, to kill and eat them. Centipedes are predators that hunt spiders. Spiders, in turn, are predators that hunt insects.

A living carpet

As the months pass, the log settles into its new role on the forest floor. Slowly, a living carpet of mosses and lichens grows over its old bark. These small plants trap rain and dew, creating damp places that attract animals like snails and leeches. The trapped water soaks through the bark, and the log gradually begins to rot or decay.

▽ *Mosses and lichens slowly cover the log in a living carpet, creating a damp habitat.*

△ *Leeches can live only in damp places. If their delicate bodies dry out, they die.*

△ *Snails are cool customers. They feed at night, when the air is cool and moist.*

WHAT ROT!

Rot is good! Rot is the best recycler on Earth.

Imagine the mountains of dead plants and animals that would have covered this planet over millions of years if the process of decay (rot) hadn't cleaned them away. All living things, however large, are recycled when they die so that the **nutrients** (food) in their bodies can feed other plants and animals.

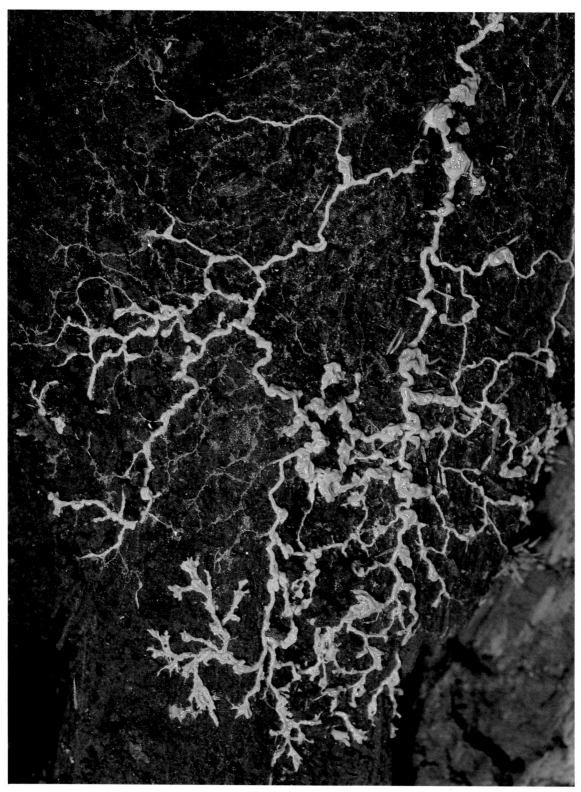

△ *A yellow slime mould threads its way across the log, feeding as it goes.*

Spreading the rot

Have you ever wondered what makes things rot? Rot is caused by fungi and microscopic bacteria that feed on dead plants and animals.

Fungi thrive in damp, dark places. Their minute threads (called hyphae) are soon spreading along hidden cracks in the log, feeding as they go.

If you looked at the rotting wood under a microscope you would see that the hyphae aren't feeding alone. Bacteria are also helping to spread the rot.

▽ *This is the part of the fungus that you don't see. It's made up of fine threads (hyphae) that creep through the wood, feeding and helping to spread the rot. Mushrooms and toadstools are only the 'fruit' of the fungi.*

DID YOU KNOW?

Fungi are neither plants nor animals. Though they look rather like plants, they are put in a separate group of their own.

Green plants contain chlorophyll, which helps them make their own food using minerals, carbon dioxide, water and energy from the sun. Fungi have no chlorophyll; they draw nutrients (food) from rotting wood and other decaying matter.

When the fungi are ready to multiply, toadstools start popping up out of the rotting wood. Their job is to make microscopic spores that will grow into new fungi.

Some spores hitch a ride on the wind, or on insects or slugs and snails. They are carried to other parts of the forest where their life cycle can begin again. Others use different transport.

The cooler, wet autumn weather that helps the toadstools to sprout has made a Bush Rat very hungry; the insects it likes are hard to find. Tonight it's lucky. It finds an orange toadstool, and takes it to a safe place to eat.

The toadstool is lucky, too. Although it is eaten, its spores spill out along the ground and over other logs, as the rat carries it away. New fungi will grow from these scattered spores.

▷ *A hungry Bush Rat finds some toadstools. They could be poisonous to us, but the rat can safely eat them.*

◁ *These toadstools are the 'fruit' of hidden fungi. They produce the millions of microscopic spores that grow into new fungi.*

DID YOU KNOW?

Plants produce fruit and seeds. An apple is a fruit, and its pips are the seeds of a new apple tree.

In fungi, mushrooms and toadstools are like the fruit, and **spores** are like the seeds. Many toadstools are poisonous to people, but not to all animals.

The demolition squad

△ *Termites (sometimes called 'white ants') are not ants at all, but quite different insects. Mouthful by mouthful they help to recycle fallen trees in the forest.*

Other important visitors to the rotting log are termites. Termites eat wood. If they get into the timber beams of a house they cause great damage. But in the forest they play a very important role in recycling.

Mouthful by mouthful, tiny, blind termites have been chewing their way through dead trees for about one hundred million years.

You might wonder how the termites in our forest will find the log which is nearly fifty metres from their nest. These termites make tunnels through the soil. The tunnels radiate out from the nest, so it doesn't take the workers long to find a new log in their territory. They start chewing into it from underneath, and tunnel through to its centre. You wouldn't know they were there unless you broke open the log.

△ *This beetle grub is busy chewing the log's hardest wood into sawdust.*

▽ *The bush cockroach, another little eating-machine, is helping to demolish the log.*

Other little eating-machines, such as beetles, grubs and bush cockroaches, also help to recycle the log. They chew holes in the hard wood, leaving sawdust everywhere. Fungi follow their tracks into the log. Earthworms find the sawdust and carry it down into the soil.

The night hunters

The log is a store-room of fresh food: tasty termites, crunchy beetles, juicy worms and lizards. The demolition workers and their neighbours could soon be in trouble—their enemies (the predators) know where to find them. Each night the log is raided; tunnel walls crumble, ripped open by strong claws.

A King Cricket finds an easy meal—a helpless grub that was living in the rotting wood. But the cricket will have to be careful; it just as easily could end up as someone else's dinner.

▽ *As the log becomes home to more grubs, spiders and other creepy crawlies, predators come to the log to feed on them.*

▷ *A King Cricket raids the log and soon makes a meal of a fat, white grub.*

△ *This gecko will make a feast of termites whenever it can find them.*

A gecko makes a quick meal of termites. You might think this gecko is licking its lips at the thought of all those termites. In fact it's licking its eyeballs! Geckoes can't blink, so they lick their eyes clean with their tongue.

Sometimes, at dusk, a very different hunter visits the log. It's covered with long, sharp quills, and has strong claws and a long, sticky tongue which are just the right tools for catching ants and termites—it's an Echidna.

△ *To an Echidna, the rotting log is like a storeroom full of its favourite food—termites!*

▷ *The Echidna's long, sticky tongue is perfect for licking tasty termites out of their long, narrow tunnels.*

Not all the night hunters come from other parts of the forest. Some have actually moved into the log.

A Funnel-web Spider has made her home deep in the soft wood, and lined the walls with silk. She has fixed trip lines radiating out from the entrance. During the day, she and her babies hide deep in the burrow, safe from birds and other predators. At night, she sits just inside the entrance and waits for dinner to walk by.

As soon as a small animal touches one of her silk trip lines, she feels the vibrations and rushes out to grab it.

Another fascinating predator lives in the damp, crumbling wood. Biologists call it Peripatus. Its common name is Velvet Worm.

You might expect these delicate creatures to feed on plants and rotting vegetation—to be herbivores. But no, they are carnivores that hunt small spiders, crickets and unwary beetles. Any one of these could eat a Velvet Worm, but Peripatus knows how to catch without being caught. Its ancestors were hunting long before the dinosaurs roamed the earth, and before spiders and insects came along.

Velvet Worms shoot their prey. They fire jets of sticky slime from glands on each side of their head. Once the victim is trapped under a sticky net, the Velvet Worm can move in for the kill.

Sometimes it shoots in self-defence. A faceful of glue stops most enemies and gives the Velvet Worm time to escape.

◁ *A Funnel-web Spider sits in the entrance to her burrow in the log, waiting for dinner.*

▽ *A Velvet Worm uses the mossy log as a home and a hunting ground. It traps its prey under a net of sticky glue.*

△ *This wonderful egg, found amongst the rotting wood, was a mystery. None of the scientists who saw it could guess what might hatch from it. But on Christmas morning the riddle was solved. Seven tiny leeches emerged—it was a leech cocoon.*

▽ *Many predators would eat skink eggs, if they could find them, so the mother skink scratches out a safe place in the crumbling old log.*

The nursery

Through the seasons, the rotting log provides a home, a food store and a hunting ground for many animals. It is also a nursery.

Eggs are extremely important! They contain the future of their species. Each mother takes great care to lay her eggs in the place that will give them the best chance of hatching. For some animals, our log is just the right place.

Wood-boring beetles tunnel into the log to lay their eggs. When the grubs hatch, they are surrounded by the wood they need to eat.

Skinks and other lizards scratch out places for their eggs in the humus. Humus keeps the eggs at the right temperature and stops them drying out. It also hides them from predators.

Eggs are helpless; they can't move themselves out of danger. The mother skink hides her eggs, because she won't be staying around to look after them.

DID YOU KNOW?

Humus is the soft, crumbling material left when plants and animals decay. It's like the compost we use in the garden. It's rich in nutrients (food) that help plants to grow.

◁ *Here's another cocoon; it belongs to an earthworm. Leeches and earthworms place their eggs, and a supply of food for the babies, inside these tiny cocoons. They hide them in moist, dark places where they won't dry out.*

Snails and slugs lay their delicate eggs in damp places under the log. These eggs don't have shells to protect them. If they dry out, or get too wet, they die. It's a wonder any hatch at all!

Some animals do guard their eggs, and look after their young.

The sight of a Huntsman Spider sitting over her egg sac is enough to frighten off most enemies. When the spiderlings hatch, they cluster around their mother's long, hairy legs for some days. She provides them with safety and food.

Centipedes also take care of their eggs. A mother centipede scrapes out a place in the decaying log and lays her eggs there. Then she wraps her body around them and guards them from hungry mouths. When the helpless babies hatch, she stays wrapped around them. It will be days before they are ready to take their chances in the wild.

DID YOU KNOW?

Life in the wild is dangerous. Many animals in the log end up as food for someone else, but at least some will grow up and have their own young. In this way, their species can survive. If there are not enough adults to breed, the species eventually becomes extinct. They are lost for ever.

△ Like many animals, snails and slugs hide their eggs where they have the best chance of hatching. There is no mother to protect this little slug when it hatches.

◁ A mother centipede guards her babies until they are ready to take their chances in the wild.

▷ A Huntsman Spider keeps watch over her egg sac.

The gardeners

lowly, year by year, the plants and animals in and around the log cause many changes. Eventually the log collapses, riddled with the holes of wood-boring insects, chewed by termites and grubs, rotted by bacteria and fungi. They all help to turn the log's hard wood into a crumbling heap.

A goanna comes scratching around the ruins of the log and turns up insects, geckoes and earthworms. Small birds fly down and steal what they can. The goanna uses its strong legs and claws to break open any large bits of rotting wood that are left. Inside, it finds the last fat beetle grub.

▽ *Now the old log is just a crumbling heap. A goanna rakes through the ruins and finds one last juicy grub.*

△ *A Brush-turkey, scratching for seeds and insects, churns the rotten wood into the soil.*

Later in the day, a Brush-turkey comes across the goanna's diggings. It scratches here and scratches there, churning, turning, searching: mixing the rotting wood and soil as it goes.

You might say that the Brush-turkey and the goanna are like gardeners, digging the rotting compost into the soil.

The cycle of life

The story of the rotten log is almost over. Bacteria, fungi and other organisms keep feeding on bits of wood scattered through the soil, breaking them down into even smaller bits. Earthworms carry them deeper into the soil, mixing them with rotting leaves and other material to make a wonderful compost—food for the plants of the forest.

Long ago, when the log was still a tree, its green leaves used the sun's energy to make its own food. Caterpillars ate some of these leaves. When they digested the leaves, they were using the food made by the tree—you could say they turned the leaves into caterpillars. Then along came birds that ate some caterpillars—you could say they turned the caterpillars into birds.

This is what we call the food web. Just as the living tree was part of the food web, the dead tree—the rotting log—is part of the same web.

Autumn has come to the forest once more. Ripening clusters of orange berries decorate the bushes. Parrots fly into the treetops to feed on the red and purple fruits. At night, Bush Rats and marsupial mice eat the fruits that have fallen to the ground.

In exchange for food, the animals help the plants. When the birds fly off with the fruit, or the mammals take it back to their nests, they carry the plants' seeds to new places in the forest.

DID YOU KNOW?

All plants and animals (all living things) are part of the **food web.** The nutrients and energy stored in their bodies are passed on to other plants and animals. It's an endless cycle that has been going on since life began on Earth.

△ Autumn fruits start to rippen in the forest.

▷ A shy Bush Rat nibbles berries; a change from toadstools and grasshoppers.

A new beginning

One bright red fruit has fallen into a small heap of soil. Within weeks it has germinated (begun to grow), and the tiny seedling is growing up towards the sunlight. And so the cycle is complete: a new tree is growing in the forest, taking its food from the compost that was once the old tree.

Index

For H.H.B. and Foxground, with thanks.

© Text and photographs, Kathie Atkinson, 1993

This book is copyright under the Berne Convention.
No reproduction without permission. All rights reserved.

A Little Ark Book
First published 1993
Allen & Unwin Pty Ltd
9 Atchison Street, St Leonards
NSW 2065, Australia

10 9 8 7 6 5 4 3 2

National Library of Australia
Cataloguing-in-Publication entry:

Atkinson, Kathie.
    Life in a rotten log.

    ISBN 1 86373 330 2.
    ISBN 1 86373 329 9. (pbk.).

    1. Tree trunks - Juvenile literature.
    2. Tree trunks - Pictorial works - Juvenile literature.
    I. Title. (Series : Atkinson, Kathie. Wild books).

591.160495

Designed by Sandra Nobes
Typeset by P.I.X.E.L Pty Ltd, Melbourne
Printed by McPherson's Printing Group, Victoria